Expressions from My Heart Continued

Veronica R. Neblett

authorHOUSE®

AuthorHouse™
1663 Liberty Drive
Bloomington, IN 47403
www.authorhouse.com
Phone: 833-262-8899

Published by AuthorHouse   12/06/2021

ISBN: 978-1-4389-0783-3 (sc)

Print information available on the last page.

Scripture taken from the King James Version of the Bible.

Scripture taken from the Holy Bible, New International Version®*. Copyright* © *1973,
1978, 1984 Biblica. Used by permission of Zondervan. All rights reserved.*

Scripture taken from the Holy Bible, New International Version®*. Copyright* © *1973,
1978, 1984 Biblica. Used by permission of Zondervan. All rights reserved.*

*Scripture taken from the New Revised Standard Version Bible, copyright 1989,
Division of Christian Education of the National Council of the Churches of Christ
in the United States of America. Used by permission. All rights reserved.*

The Living Bible copyright © *1971 by Tyndale House Foundation. Used
by permission of Tyndale House Publishers Inc., Carol Stream, Illinois
60188. All rights reserved. The Living Bible, TLB, and the The Living
Bible logo are registered trademarks of Tyndale House Publishers.*

*Any people depicted in stock imagery provided by Getty Images are models,
and such images are being used for illustrative purposes only.
Certain stock imagery* © *Getty Images.*

This book is printed on acid-free paper.

Contents

III. Relationships

IV. Praise and Worship

Many thanks $2.00 of the purchase price of this book will be donated
to Straight Pathway Ministry. www.straightpathwayministries.com

Author's Thoughts

God has truly blessed me. As I sit and remember all God has done for me I cannot help but praise Him. He has shown His love in so many ways, through his care for me, my children, my grandchildren, and my family. Through many healings, He has given me in my body, soul, and spirit.

Who is man that God is mindful of him? What a question, we are the products of His creation made in His likeness. And He loved us so much He was willing to give of Himself (Jesus) to bring us back into right relationship with Him.

We have heard so many times that God is good, but what do we mean. I mean that He is Love, Sovereign, Merciful and Superior to all other so so-called gods. He is the God who created all that we see. He is the God that said after creating man and all He had made was very good.

If you don't know God, accept Him now and believe the work His Son Jesus Christ did on Calvary's cross. Acknowledge and repent of your sins and He who is faithful will forgive you and give you the <u>gift</u> of the Holy Spirit to lead and guide you in this walk with Him.

As you read this book think on the goodness of God and all He has done for us and you will say like me, what an Awesome God we serve.

Be blessed,

Veronica R. Neblett

Dedication

A lot of this second volume was inspired by my pastor, Bishop George Brooks. He has truly been a blessing in my life and my family. He is God's man for this last hour. I would be remiss if I left out his wife, First Lady Edna Brooks for she is an example of a woman of God.

I dedicate this also to my children, Debra and Preston Neblett who God gave me to care for and teach His ways; my prayer for them is that they always put God first in their lives. I challenge them both to be all that God has created them to be.

I cannot leave out my grandchildren, Arkel and Deja' who have been a blessing in my life. I pray they will always put God first and be all that God has created them to be.

Veronica R. Neblett

Foreword

Veronica Neblett has elevated the intensity from which she draws out of her in <u>Expressions from My Heart Continued</u>. The insightfulness is certainly practical yet divine. It addresses our humanity through the eyes of a divine and loving God. She will challenge you to not only recognize God, but on institute all the things that he has commissioned us to do after seeing Him. You cannot help but experience his presence as you read line after line. You cannot help but ask yourself the question. "Why didn't I think of that?"

As the Bible declares, out of the heart flows the issue of life these poems not only describe life, but also describe the source. I encourage you to read and reread these poems in all situations. When you are depressed, they will inspire you. Finally, when you would have read through enough times, they will change you.

Bishop George W. Brooks
Pastor Emeritus
Mount Zion Baptist Church, Inc.
Greensboro, North Carolina

Nature

Remembering His Awesomeness

Psalms 93:1a "The Lord reigns, he is robed in majesty; the Lord is
robed in majesty and is armed with strength…" (NIV)

It's amazing; looking at the ocean remembering the parting of the Red Sea
and how God told Moses to just lift his rod and the sea departed.

When I look at world issues today and say what are they compared to the
power of GOD to speak, and change occurs.

It was YOU, who created man in Your image, gave us dominion over the
earth and said be fruitful and multiply.

God knowing the future and the hearts of man said, "If my people who
are called by my name would humble themselves and pray, seek God's face,
turn from their sinful ways then will I hear from heaven and forgive their
sins and heal their land" (2Ch 7:14).

Why should we worry and fret when we serve a Sovereignty such as YOU,
who reigns forever with majesty and power.

As the ocean air clears my thoughts, I clearly see Your purpose for man
and what you require of us and I say thy will be done.

Lord, help us to always keep in mind Your greatness and power and that
You still sit on Your throne.

Beautiful Waves of Contentment

As I stood looking at the power of the ocean waves, I said, "What an awesome God You are."

As the waves moved back and forth my spirit calmed, my questions began to fade with each movement of the water.

The water is clear and the radiance from the sun beats upon the waves as I envision the greatness of Your countenance,

As the waves move over the ocean Your Spirit brings great peace to my heart, mind, and spirit.

As the waves swept over the sand and made all the grains smooth, Your Spirit swept over the grainy areas of my life and made them smooth.

The waves varied in size just like the chastisement You chose to keep me in Your divine will, why? Because You love me and Your plans for me are always good to give me an expected end.

As the waves obeyed Your will my heart says yes, your grace is sufficient, who else knows how to genuinely care for me, but Thee.

As the sun goes down and the waves move closer in land and claims it for the night so does Your LOVE as You watch over my soul each night.

Oh, what beautiful waves of contentment.

Coolness of the Wind is God's Presence

As I sit on the beach, I feel the coolness of the wind.

A feeling of peace and purpose has filled my mind.

God's peace has such a settling in the inner man.

I know God's purpose for my life.

I know where He's taking me and what He desires to accomplish in me.

I must yield to Him daily and rebuke the enemy, who desires to taunt my mind with fear.

I know for sure that God is moving in and around me.

God's mercy is ever upon me moving me in the direction of His promise.

I will die daily of my will and live for His purpose.

The coolness of the wind is God's presence for me today.

"Katrina", Can you hear God?

Jeremiah 29:11-12 (KJV) "For surely I know the plans I have for you, says the Lord, plans for your welfare and not for harm, to give you a future with hope. Then when you call upon me and come and pray to me, I will hear you".

Katrina, "Do you hear God?"
He has been swinging His Rod.
God spoke clear to us that day.
Hoping we would repent and pray.

Katrina gathers her strength and hits with a bang.
Man, in his finite knowledge thought he knew the plan.
God is trying to reason with man.
That's why in love He lifted His hand.

Katrina caused lost, pain, suffering and death.
Destroying some of the areas of wealth,
God is tired of sin running rampant in the land.
We have not seen anything, if we do not heed God's Commands.

God destroyed two cities because of sin.
What makes man think today they can win?
Repent, trust in God and make your stand.
God will not always show His Mercy to man.

Watch, how you throw your ability in God's face.
He still has the power and the strength to erase.
Don't be like Nimrod; he thought he could build to the sky.
Trusting in himself with each brick he supplied.
Nimrod thought he was the boss.
But with each command the language was lost.

God showed us we could not trust in man.
The people were stranded calling out for a hand.
We saw our country not at her best.
Struggling to help but failing the test.

Some say, "Why would God allow this to be?"
God says, "I gave my Son for thee."
We heard many cry out for help.
God knew just how they felt.

Katrina, "Do you hear God?"
What can we get from all of this?
Trust in God you will never miss.

Life's Experiences

False Evidence Appearing Real (FEAR)

I John 4:18 "Perfect love cast out all fear…." (KJV)

Fear is a taunting spirit from hell that works in the mind of man.
Fear is used to rob God's people of their victory.
Fear has no place among God's people.
Fear prevents man from his divine purpose in God.

Fear must be broken that's a fact;
Fear is a tool use to keep us back.
Don't allow fear to keep you in lack.
Fear must leave in the name of Jesus.

God has given us the victory we must stand on it and be free.
God has purposed this for us can't you see.
God has given us the power to put Satan under our feet.
God has given us power over all of Satan scams
Trusts in God remain in His hands.

Resist the devil he will flee; trust in God you will see.
There is no weapon formed against that can prosper.
God has given us victory and we are more than conquerors.

Don't let the devil rob your joy.
Don't let him play you like a toy.
Don't let fear keep you back,
Trust God to keep your mind on track.

When fear comes to taunt your mind,
Tell the devil to get behind
Perfect love cast out all fear,
Trust in God and the devil will disappear.

Listen to God's will for thee…

John 10:4 (NKJV) "And when he brings out his own sheep, he goes
before them; and the sheep follow him, for they know his voice".

The enemy is a defeated force he has no power over God's people. His
tactics are deceitful and undercover, but God has given us the VICTORY.
All we must do is pass the test God will do the rest.

God's says to us I am with you, I see your struggles, I hear your prayers,
I see your desires to serve me and win souls.
He says to us you are more than a conqueror.
I have purpose for you in these last days, hold on I will use you mightily
to tear down the devil's kingdom.

Fear not I am with thee; I have you in my hands no matter how it seems.
I am molding and making you for my use.
Fear not, trust me, I am God of My word,
Continue to yield to Me daily, as I meet your needs.

There is a price to pay for the anointing that is desired of ME,
Stand still, and allow Me to mold and make you
No weapon formed against you shall prosper.
I have you and am instilling in you what you need to bind up the broken
hearted and bring liberty to the captive and teach My people MY truth.

These are the days of completing what I have begun in thee,
Don't fear the enemy when he shows up because he has no power over you.
Trust ME, seek ME, and stay in MY word. It's your weapon against the
forces of darkness.

I will order your steps as you yield to ME. I see your heart, I know your
desire, and I know your faithfulness to MY kingdom. Stay strong in the
Lord and in the power of HIS might.

Journey with God

Isn't it wonderful how we want to share the blessings of God with others? But God is saying not now, I'm dealing with you.

Sometimes we want to take others along on our journey with God. But God is saying not now, walk alone. He desires to deal with us individually not as a group.

A one on one lesson is needed at times. God wants to mold us into the image He desires for us, and the voices of others interfere with what God is saying.

On this journey, God's presence, sometimes is overwhelming to the point of fear but I know He loves us and He's just near

At times, we can't express how we feel but we know that it's God because there is an atmosphere of love and peace.

When the journey with God ends, we are ready to move into our purpose with wisdom, knowledge and understanding, because we have allowed God to mold and make us into a vessel of honor, ready for His use.

Allow your journey with God to begin. It's for your good..........

Beware of Praise

Calvary was a lonely road,
Jesus died and His story was told.

It all started one beautiful sunny day.
Jesus entered the city of Jerusalem on a donkey you see.
Palm branches were thrown at His feet.
The people were jubilant as they shouted,
Hosanna, Hosanna he's Our Lord and King.

What happened during that week?
A secret trial at night you see.
And the Jewish leaders' treachery
They cursed His name all that night.
The voices shouted crucify Him, he's not right
The accusation they shouted were not kind,
The secret trial caused evil minds

Jesus did good everywhere he went,
He healed the sick, he raised the dead,
He showed love to all He met.
Some called Him, "Lord, teacher and friend"

Less than a week had passed and now some say,
"Crucify Him, crucify Him, we don't believe He's the way."
"We don't believe He came from God."
"Who is this Jesus? He's not our King!"

Jesus was crucified on the cross.
He rose the third day, thank God, we don't have to be lost.
The story is not over, can't you see,
Repent and believe and He will set you free.

Beware of those who speak good,
Make sure you know what's under their hood.
Beware of praise know the source,
Don't get confused or you will be loss.

You

YOU desire us to obey and follow as YOU lead.

As I sit waiting on YOU to speak to my heart
I'm grateful for what YOU have already done in me.

No, I don't know what way to turn or what to do until YOU speak,
But I do know that I'm empty without YOU and can do nothing
without YOU.

It's in YOU I move, live and have my being.
It's YOU, who places the desire to live righteous and obey.

As I remember the scripture that says how wonderful are your works,
I think of the work YOU have done in me.

At times I am not sure of the road I must take to fulfill my purpose,
But one thing I do know is that I will not be traveling it without YOU.

Tell me, how can God use us if we don't pray?

"Pray without ceasing". I Thessalonians 5:17 (KJV)

Prayer meeting night,
Very few leaders in sight
My heart is grieved when I look around,
And there were few leaders to be found.
We stand in the pulpit and say let's meet for prayer,
But where are you when it's time to share.
How do we hope to build our relationship with God without fellowship
in prayer?
How can we be effective in ministry without a prayer life?
How can we lead others to Christ if we don't pray and seek God's face?
How can we tell others to pray if we don't lead by example?
How can God use us if we don't pray and ask Him how to win souls?
Are we seeking God's face and praying or are we just promoting prayer?

Oh, how grieved I was to see that God's people don't desire to get closer
to Him in prayer. I am mere man think of how God felt. God is tired of
all mouth and no power to back it up. We hear all the time that there is
a great falling away from the Church. But where are we when it's time to
seek God's face.

The Bible states, that man ought to always pray and not faint.
What's wrong with the saints?
Prayer is where we gain our strength to fight off the devil and gain victory,
Wake up church before it's too late.
Don't let God find us out of place,
Pray and seek His face.

Tell me, how can God use us if we don't pray?

Walking Alone

I have chosen you to walk alone,
Don't be afraid trust in God he will set the tone.

It's hard at time it seems like a test,
But God has chosen you and He knows what's best.

I try to blend in with the crowd,
God's discernment shows me their hearts.

Why can't man be what they preach?
And treat each other with the love they teach.

God has chosen me that's a fact,
Truth is in me I don't have to act.

Who is to say where God takes me from here,
One thing for sure God will be there.

God has chosen me for this task,
I will trust in Him and not wear a mask.

Walking alone is not that bad,
Because God's presence surrounds me and I am truly glad.

I'm not alone for God is there,
His word tells me He's everywhere.

The Wind Shall Not Win!

Isaiah 26:18a "but we gave birth to the wind". Isaiah 66:14 "You shall see, and
your heart shall rejoice; your bodies' shall flourish like the grass; and it shall
be known that the hand of the Lord is with his servants…" (NRSV)

We shall not give birth to the wind.
God will bring forth babies of His kind.
God shall show us the things we do not know.
And when God is finished we will glow.

Only God understands the needs of man.
We must learn to place them in His capable hand.
From the beginning, God knew what was best for us.
If we would only forget our ideas, believe His Word and trust.

God created us in His image and likeness,
And told us to be fruitful and multiply.
God's Plan from the beginning was good for us.
God's ways are far higher than ours and His thoughts are always just.

God has taken us through too much to let His vision fail.
Obey God's Word and victory will prevail.
The vision God has is far beyond our abilities or capabilities.
Trust and believe God, He will show us possibilities.

Lean on God and His Sovereignty to lead and direct us our
hope must remain in God.
We must obey Him and not depart.
With unity, we have strength to tear the devil's kingdom down.
But our unity must be with purity of hearts and minds.

God has spoken and we have no excuse.
Listen to God and do not take the devil's abuse.
We do not want God's Spirit to turn away.
We must trust, believe and obey.

God's Word will not come back void.
Pray, yield to God and seek to know His Perfect Will.
Victory will be ours, if we let ourselves be still.
No, we shall not give birth to the wind.
We shall give birth to babies, strong, armed and ready to be used by God.
NO, THE WIND SHALL NOT WIN…

What is Christmas?

"For unto us a Child is born, Unto us a Son is given; And the government
will be upon His shoulder. And His name will be called Wonderful,
Counselor, Mighty God, Everlasting Father, Prince of Peace"
(Isaiah 6:9 KJV).

Christmas is a day of celebration for all God has given to us,
Christmas is not how big your gift is and all the fuss.
Christmas is another time of remembering that a kingly child was born,
Christmas is a time of remembering that This child would grow
up and be scorned.

Christmas is not about the things that man has done,
Christmas is a day to remember that God gave His Son.
Isn't it funny how we change the meaning of this day
Forgetting that God sent His Son to show us the way

Yes, Jesus is the reason for this season.
Do not let His birth be just another day of strife,
Remember that it was Him who died and gave us new life.

As families gather to eat and chew the fat,
Let us pause and thank God for not turning His back.
For God so loved the world He gave His Son.
Jesus was crucified and the weight of our sins felt like a ton.
Though our sins prevented the Father from looking upon His Son,
Jesus' death meant the victory was won.

Daughter/Son, I AM with Thee

"And, lo, I am with you always, even until the end of the world" Matt: 28:20b KJV

I know this trial you are in seems hard,
But God has been with you from the start.
Do not be discouraged; keep your mind above,
Believe in ME, I AM the God of LOVE.
When it gets hard and your head drops down,
Remember Jesus healed all over town.

Don't let the devil try to take you out,
Remember who I AM, lift your hands and shout.
You might ask, "Why me for this test?"
Because you can count on God's best.
It might look dark from day to day,
But I AM the one who lights your way.

Your body might be weak and you may think can I get it back?
Yes, you can if you stay on track.
You might say, "Father, how long must this be?"
He says, "Why, AM I not with thee?"
Was it not my Son they nailed to the cross?"
Jesus stayed there that you might not be lost.

"Lift your head up I know it seems hard.
I have been with you from the start."

Singleness is caring for the Things of the Lord

"But I would have you without carefulness. He that is unmarried careth
for the things of the Lord, how he may please the Lord (I Cor.7:32 KJV).
Thou will show me the path of life; in thy presence is fullness of joy; at
thy right hand, there are pleasures for evermore" (Psalm 16:11)

We often forget the good things about the single life,
Because we are too busy trying to be a husband or a wife.
Turn your focus to God and His plans,
In your singleness, you can dedicate more time to be a witness to man.

God create us to glorify and praise His name,
Being single helps you not to be average or the same.
Lift your head up and declare Gods word,
Be loyal be faithful and trust in the Lord.

Your completion is not based on having a woman or man.
But knowing who God is and following His commands.
The enemy is out to kill and destroy,
But in God's presence is the fullness of joy.

We hear a lot today about finding your soul mate,
Set up time for prayer and ask God to be your date.
God has challenged man to run this race,
Be concern about God's things and He will set the pace.

Singleness is caring about the things of the Lord,
Hoping one day to reign with Him above.
Do not lose hope ask God to keep you on the right track,
Remembering that He knows your needs and He has your back.

Man's Ego

Man's ego divides God's people.
God has called us to unity.
Jesus prayed to the Father to make us one,
Just like the Father and the Son.

Tell me what we can do without God.
Can we heal the sick?
Can we raise the dead? No!
So, why does man allow his ego to rule his life?

It's in You that we move, live and have our being, not us.
Trusting and relying on you is a must.
Man's ego must be destroyed,
God's purpose must be fulfilled.

We must place ourselves in God's hand.
And pray that God delivers the ego of man.
We must fight against this spirit that divides.
And remember it's the Father that will always provide.

You can make a Difference

"Even the righteousness of God which is by faith of Jesus Christ unto all and upon all them that believe: for there is no difference" (Romans 3:22 KJV).

You can make a difference that's what I say,
You can make a difference if God leads the way.
You might say I don't know how to win souls;
You can learn when heaven is your goal.

One might say what difference I can possibly make,
You can make a difference when your relatives and friends
lives are at stake.
Winning a soul to some is not an easy task,
But it can be easy if you are not wearing a mask.

Our own daily walk with Christ we say is enough,
Be kind be gentle and free yourself of arrogant stuff.
Walk in the Spirit of God's love each and everyday,
Believing that Christ will show you victory if you don't sway.

Be willing to forgive and forget the things you experience in the past,
And remember it's only what you do for Christ will last.
You can Make a Difference in the land,
Just trust in God and heed His command.

Inspired by: Bishop George Brooks
By: Veronica Neblett
1/26/2008

Relationships

Recipe for Eternal Life

<u>Ingredients</u>

1. 1 cup: Romans 6:23 KJV "For the wages of sin is death but the gift of God is eternal life"

2. 1 cup: Romans 3:23 KJV "We all have sinned and come short of the glory of God"

3. 1 cup: Romans 5: 8 KJV "God showed His love towards us that when we were yet in sin He died for us"

4. 1 cup: Romans 10:9 KJV "If you would confess with your mouth the Jesus is Lord and believe in your heart that God raised Jesus from the dead, ye shall be saved".

Heat the oven to John 3:16 KJV "For God so love the world that He gave His only begotten Son, that whosoever believeth in Him should not perish, but have everlasting life".

Now take # 1 and #2 and mix it with I John 1:9 KJV "If we would confess our sins, he is faithful and just to forgive us our sins, and to cleanse us from all unrighteousness".

Mix in # 3 and# 4 with the essence of prayer until you receive Acts 2:38a KJV "But ye shall receive power, after the Holy Ghost is come upon you".

Put yourself in the oven until you are persuaded that neither death, nor life, nor angels, nor principalities, nor powers, nor things present, nor things to come, nor heights, nor depth, nor any other creature, shall be able to separate you from the love of God, which is in Christ Jesus our Lord. (Rom: 8:38,39 KJV) .

Take yourself out the oven and cool down, remembering the promise of Christ in John 14:1-3 KJV "Let not your heart be troubled; ye believe in God, believe also in me. In my Father's house are many mansions, if it were not so, I would have told you, I go to prepare a place for you. And if I go and prepare a place for you, I will come again, and receive you unto myself, that where I am, there ye may be also".

Top it off with Jude: 24,25 KJV "Now unto him that is able to keep you from falling, and to present you faultless before the presence of his glory with exceeding joy, To the only wise God our Savior, be glory and majesty, dominion and power, both now and ever. Amen.

Wonderful Jesus

Wonderful Jesus that's your name,
I will never be the same.

Wonderful Jesus brought me out,
I can dance unto Him and shout.

Wonderful Jesus that's my King,
I will always love Him and sing.

Wonderful Jesus there is none like you,
I will always trust and be true.

Wonderful Jesus that's all I can say,
I will love and obey Him every day.

Wonderful Jesus that's your name,
I thank God; I'll never be the same.

Jesus Prayed for Us

John 17:9 "I pray for them, I do not pray for the world but for those whom You have given Me, for they are Yours". KJV

Jesus knelt and looked up to the Father and prayed for us,
His mouth was filled with love and trust.
He asks the Father not to take them out of the world,
But strengthen them to triumph over every test.

Father I told them of your sacrificing love,
And how You sent ME from above.
Father I lift them up to thee alone,
Knowing that it's YOU who sits on the throne.

I obeyed your will and was nailed to the cross,
My blood allows your children not to be loss.
Who can pluck them out of your hands?
When they trust, and obey your commands.

The enemy is trying to destroy all God has created, especially man,
But Jesus death and resurrection gave us the power to stand.
Father you put all power in MY hand,
The devil's tricks will never destroy your plan

Not MY will but thine be done.
For you have chosen me to die your Son
The Father sent the Comforter to lead and guide,
Who better to stand by man's side?

Jesus thanked the Father for sending His best,
Jesus prayers were answered your children can eternally rest.

Be still, "It is I"

Psalm 46:10 "Be still, and know that I am God; I will be exalted among the nations, I will be exalted in the earth"! KJV

Be still and know that I am God,
It is I, who has created all things.

It is I, who will open blinded eyes,
It is I, who will lift heavy burdens.

It is I, who will open the ears of the deaf,
It is I, who will bring salvation to the loss.

It is I, who can heal all disease,
It is I, whose blood washed away all sin.

It is I, who will cause nations to bow to ME,
It is I, who will set all mankind free.

Be still my child, be still my child,
I am with thee; it is I.

Blind Trust

Psalm 56: 3 "Whenever I am afraid I will trust in YOU" KJV

Trust is hard even when you can see,
Imagine if you were blind how would that be,
Our trust in God must be as if we are blind,
God will always be on time,
It's easy to say, "Lord I trust you when you can see the way",
But what happens when God is not seen day by day,

God will always make a way of escape,
Believe in God just wait,
I can sense God's presence during the storm,
My trust in Him will keep me from all harm,

I see Jesus arms stretched wide for me,
As He hung on Calvary,
Many thought He hung His head in shame,
But I know His death was not in vain,
We must walk by faith and not by sight,
Knowing God is just and always right,

The world says that justice is blind,
But, wait on God He will give you a sign,
The Bible is clear about God's will for us,
You can stand on God's word and have blind trust.

God's Love Surrounds Thee

Psalm 24:1 "The earth is the Lord's and all its fullness: The
world and those who dwell therein". KJV

God's love surrounds me each day,
As I walk and live His way,

Have you ever thought about the sky, the earth and the sea?
Can't you feel God's presence with thee?
When you look at the sky so blue,
Doesn't it remind that God's love is true?

The earth is where God bend down and formed our outer shell,
His Son's blood was shed for us and it's a story we can tell,
God breathe in us and gave us life,
Jesus is the only way and He paid the price,

Look at how the clouds form in the sky,
Jesus sacrifice was not a lie
Go down to the ocean it's bigger than the sea,
And remember God's Love Surrounds thee.

On the other side of the Storm

Mark 4:39 "Then He arose and rebuke the wind, and said to the sea, "Peace, be still!" And the wind ceased and there was a great calm". NKJV

When the storms of life seem too much to bear,
Always stand on God's love knowing He cares,
Man, will try to discourage you that's a fact,
But, keep your mind on God and don't look back,

At times the storm is pressing down on you hard,
But hold on God knew it from the start,
He has prepared you a way out,
Lift, your hands, praise and shout,
Someone has said you can't make it through the next round,
Rebuke them, and say, "The devil is bound",

Gather your thoughts and press towards your goal,
And the enemy story will never be told,
Man, might say it can't be done,
Trust in God and the work of His Son,
When it seems like the storm won't let up,
Remember Jesus sacrifice and His cup,

Don't listen to man he will keep you in doubt,
The storm is nothing to God He will bring you out,
Jesus rebuked the storm on the raging sea,
On the other side of the storm is where you want to be.

Cupped in My Father's Hands

John 10:29 "My Father, who has given them to Me, is greater than all; and no one is able to snatch them out of My Father's hand". NKJV

No one can snatch me out of My Father's hands,
He cups me with His love and I know I can stand.

As the potter molds and makes me day by day,
I'll always remember My Father has made the way.

Those who live godly will suffer and go through many tests,
Remember that Jesus suffered and He was My Father's best.

Trials and tribulation are part of my walk,
My Father wants me to pray and do less talk.

My Father is just and knows how much I can bear,
The bible tells me how much He cares.

The psalmist said, "Weeping may endure for a night",
But in My Father's hands He keeps me in sight.

My Father has given me only one choice,
I must listen and know His voice.

I'll run my race and keep my stand,
Because I know I am cupped in My Father's hand.

God Speaks Daily

God speaks to us daily but not the same way. We often desire to hear from God the same way and place each day. But, God knows where we are and how to deal with us effectively each day. We must always trust that God knows what's best for us each day.

All His plans for us are good; we must keep our hearts clean before Him and remember that He knows the very intent of our hearts. He knows if we have hidden agendas, He knows if we are just going through the motions and not sincere. Be real before God and He will do all He has promised and more. The presence of God makes us come clean. His presence makes life's situation seem small because He is so great.

At times, just to say thank you Lord is enough to bring total deliverance because God sees our heart. We can't sufficiently thank God for all He's done so all we can say is thank you. Trust and don't doubt and He will touch the heart of men to submit to His will that you might be blessed.

Look around at what you see, did it seem beyond your reach at some point, but God. All we see and hope for is possible when we trust God. The things we thought were impossible to give up or maybe did not believe were wrong, once yielded to God, He revealed the truth and we were delivered.

Oh, how awesome are the ways of the Lord. The bible tells us that our thoughts are not His thoughts and our ways are not His. Therefore, we who are powerless without God must trust and yield to His infinite power, wisdom and knowledge to know what's best.

So, God speaks to what we need and where we are each day. God speaks to us but not the same way or place each day.

Never Doubt

Look at what God does for us each day,
He holds us in His arms and carry's us all the way.
Who can doubt God's ability to keep?
He watches over us each night as we sleep.

Don't trust in yourself to bring you out,
But lean on Him without a doubt.
Trust is walking backwards off a cliff not knowing when you will fall,
Believing God will catch you at the time of your call.

Who can't trust a God like this?
That catches you as you fall off a cliff.
Never doubt God's ability to be there,
Jesus death at Calvary proved He cared.

When you get discouraged and it's hard to hold on,
Remember not to doubt God still sits on the throne.

Vastness of God's Love

Who can know the vastness of your love, oh God?
Who can describe the peace of your love?
Who can tell the wonders of your love?
Who can speak words of life to us, oh God?
Who can chasten us with great love?

When I looked out over the ocean and see your greatness
and how you made room for man with an utterance of your Voice,
I can't help but say, how great thou art.
Man, and his small mind and boastfulness
can't imagine even your smallest thoughts.

How can I not love and obey you?
How can I not seek you daily?
How can I not trust you for all my needs?
How can I not see the sacrifice you made for me?
How can I not know you care for me each day?

I feel your presence even now it the midst of uncertainties.
Oh, how you loved me even in times of lack.
As I sat watching the waves and the movements of the ocean
I see you moving every obstacle that hinders my walk with you,
Knowing that the vastness of your love will take me through.

This is my time!

This is the time you have chosen to bless,
Especially when I think of how you brought me through all my tests.
Who I am at this very moment,
Goes beyond all the disappointments and torment.

Show me what you desire of me,
Show me thy will Lord and open my eyes that I might see.
Don't let me waste time pondering...
I yield to thee oh Lord. I yield to thy will.

I trust you Lord,
Show me your desires,
Show me your will,
As I stand still.
Help me to understand all that you say,
This is my time to be blessed of Thee.

God is real

When I see the beautiful black sky with the stars shining so bright.
How can we doubt God's love and kindness towards man?
How can one say there is no God and that you are not concerned about us?
We can see you in the ocean, in the waves and in the movement of the earth.
How can we doubt or deny that you are God and you hold all things together?

I am so glad you see our hearts and know who we really are
As we move throughout the day let us remember to say thank you Lord
For your mighty works and how you protect us each day
God cares even when we are acting crazy and doubting
God cares even when we forget His love.
God is real.

My Heart is yours God

My heart is yours, oh God.
Why do I doubt you?
Why can't I just trust your word?
Why can't I yield totally to you?

Help me, oh Lord to yield totally today.
Your will is truly what I desire.
Not some of the time but always.
Not just when I can't trust my own means.

God, I express my heart to you this day.
Hoping that those reading my words will also learn to trust and wait.
Only you see my heart and know my thoughts and the way I take.
You only can do the things I ask and think.

How long do I wait to understand?
My heart says I hear your commands.
Speak to me Lord show me your will,
I wait patiently and I am still.
Show me, thy will my heart is yours God,
It's your will that I never depart.
My heart is yours God.

Our Faith will be Challenged

"Wait on the Lord be of good courage and He will strengthen your heart. Wait I say on the Lord." Psalms 27:14 NKJV

Has God challenged your faith at all?
Have you accepted the challenge or call?

We must always believe God's voice,
And remember God makes the best choice.
When God speaks to our heart and mind,
Don't allow the devil to cause you to fall behind.

Whatever God says that is what He means.
Whether you understand the vision or not,
God's word is what it's all about.
Yes, the devil will come to steal your dream,
But remember God's purpose will gleam.

God does not give us a vision for no reason,
Pray and wait God knows the season.
What is faith if it has not been challenged?
God is the one who keeps His purpose in balance.
Don't try to make your own way,
Just trust in God and obey.

What God speaks will come to past,
Only God's promises will last.
Do not worry about what man might say,
God challenges us each day,
Faith must be challenged in our walk with God,
Stand on God's promises He is in charge.

Our faith will be challenged no matter how hard it seems,
Wait on God and remain on His team.
So, has your faith been challenged is what I asked,
Trust in God stick with the task,
Because only what you do for Christ will last.

God's Strength

And he said unto me, my grace is sufficient for thee: for
my strength is made perfect in weakness.
2 Corinthians 12:9 KJV

Why do I feel you so strong?
You are God and I am not alone.
Even though I fall,
You still remind me of my call.

I, God am with you through each test,
Knowing that you are not always at your best
I am God and I change not,
Trust in Me and have no doubt.

Keep your hands in My hand,
And I alone will help you stand.
You are strong when you are weak,
Even when things look bleak.

Remember I always know your heart,
And I know it's not your will to depart.
Stand strong keep your focus on where I God want you to be,
And always remember God's spirit dwells in thee.

Praise and Worship

Banners of Victory

Ps 20:5 "We will rejoice in your salvation, and in the name of our God we will set up our banners! May the Lord fulfill all your petitions." KJV

Lift your banners high don't be shy in praising God,
God granted all our petitions and gave us the victory,

Did man say it could not be done?
But God, the victory is won.

Our banners represent total answered prayers,
Rejoice and lift your banners high in the air.

Don't be ashamed to cry and shout,
We have stomped the devil out.

Don't let anyone take your praise away, lift your banners and say,
God has given us the victory today.

If anyone ask us what's that in your hand,
Tell them it's your banner and you are in God's band.

Thank you,

Dear God,

How often do you hear your name called? Each day you bend your ears towards mankind to hear their requests. I hope that you hear me today. I am not asking for anything but just saying thank you for how good you have been to me and my family.

God, you have brought us through so much over the years, thank you. You kept my family from death; you have healed sick bodies and extended life. You are a prayer answering God. I love how you go beyond our little requests and answer far above what we can ask you for.

When I look back and see how you have taken me through disappointed, misunderstandings and at some point giving up. Then I read your word and you say to me I know the plans I have for you, I smile and say thank you God.

I thank you for salvation through the work of the cross. I thank you for forgiveness and restoration. I thank you for your keeping power and the Comforter you sent to lead and guide us through life's situations. Not only have you done all of this but you constantly listen to our cries daily.

I can say like the Psalmist "As the deer thirst for water, my soul thirst for you." I remain humble before you so you can use me to build your kingdom on earth, is this not your will for us?

We can search throughout eternity and never find a God dearer than YOU. Thank you.

Jesus, Oh what a powerful name

Jesus, Oh what a powerful name,
When you walk with Him you will never be the same.
Jesus, sweeter than the honeycomb,
Jesus promised we would never be alone.

Some might not understand what Jesus did for us,
Jesus was the only sacrifice God could trust.
Jesus went to Calvary that we might win,
Jesus was the perfect lamb sent to bear our sins.

Jesus was beaten and spit upon before He was hung on the tree,
He was pierced in His side for our healing you see.
His blood washes all our sins away,
Why not receive Him today.

The Father said all power I put in your hands,
Trust and believe in Jesus make your stand.
Don't let Satan make your choice,
Believe, repent and lift your voice.

Jesus is the way man can be saved,
Believe God's word or you will be loss.
Jesus is the only way to the Father you can believe that,
Don't waste your time hearing false facts.

Every knee shall bow every tongue shall confess,
Jesus is Lord and through Him we will be blessed.
Believe in Him and you will never be the same
Jesus, Jesus, Oh what a powerful name.

God's Atmosphere is Holy

Psalm 140:13 "Surely the righteous shall give thanks to Your name;
The upright shall dwell in Your presence NKJV

True worship is holy and the Holy Spirit leads you into His holy presence.
To come into His presence, we must be willing to yield our total being
to HIM

Chorus
Fill the atmosphere with your presence, oh God
Fill the atmosphere with your presence, oh God

We bow down to the Holy God
We bow down to the Holy God
Chorus (2X)

YOU are a Holy God
YOU are a Holy God
Chorus (2X)

We humble ourselves before you, oh God
We humble ourselves before you, oh God
Chorus (2X)

His presence is here
Bow down to the Holy God
Chorus (2X)

The Majesty of God

Psalm 93:1a "The Lord reigns, He is clothed with majesty" …. NKJV

The Lord reigns, He is clothed with majesty.
Some might see Him still hanging on the cross,
But He came down that our souls would not be lost.

They took Him down to that cold grave,
He rose the third day that we might be saved.
The grave could not hold this great King down,
Because He did the will of the Father in each town.

He rides in majesty and victory is on His side,
Hold on to His promise and you will survive.
He's arrayed in majesty as He ascends to His throne,
He is a King who was found guilty but did no wrong.

Who can judge with justice and love?
Only God who sits on the throne above.
Who can compare to Him in majesty? No one!
The Lord reigns, He is clothed in majesty.

We are Always Triumphant

In Christ, we are Always Triumphant
The battle is always won.
Not because of what we have done,
But because the Father sent His Son.

Though the outward man perishes day by day,
Our inner man is renewed and strengthened as God shows the way.
Don't throw in the towel because of a minor test,
We always have the victory. We have God's best.

It matters not what man might say.
Victory is ours always.
Weeping may endure for a night,
But when morning comes victory is always bright.

The weapons of our warfare are not carnal,
We are always triumphant that's why we can marvel.
On every occasion, we always win,
Jesus died for us and we are always triumphant within.

Let no one tell you the battle is lost,
Look to Jesus, He is always our source.
What we see is temporary,
What we don't see is forever.
Keep your focus, stand your ground,
There is always victory where Christ is found.
In Christ, we are Always Triumphant.

"I Live to Serve You, Oh Lord"

"I shall not die, but live and declare the works of the Lord (Ps. 118:17) NKJV

I live to serve you that's what I say,
I live to serve you each day,
What can I do without your touch?
That is why I praise and love You so much.

No one can touch my heart like you do,
The One who keeps me and takes me through.
It's You who knows my ends and outs,
Oh Lord, you make my soul to shout.

I live to serve thee, Oh Lord,
Because you are the One I adore.
I live to serve you because there is no other way,
That's why I live to serve you each day.

I live to serve you Oh Lord!!!!

Do you know why Jesus died?

Do you know that Jesus died for you?
Don't let anyone tell you it's not true.
He suffered in the hands of man,
That's why I know we can stand.

Do you know that Jesus was slapped and spit on because of us?
That's why today salvation is a must.
His blood will wash away our sins and change our life?
It's true to all who believe and give up all strife.

When you think of all Jesus suffered that we might be free,
Why are you standing there where you should not be?
Yes, Jesus was put in a cold and borrow grave,
But not for long, He rose that we might be saved.

So, during this great time and season,
Remember that Jesus died and rose because we were the reason.
So, do you know what all this means to us,
We are without excuse and in God we must trust.

There is only one way to the Father and that's through His Son,
Repent today and your victory is won.
So now you know why Jesus died.

There is Still Room at the Cross

There is room at the cross,
Yet there are still so many who are loss.

Lord help us to bring the wayward man to Christ,
Help us to break the ice.

You are what we all need,
Help us to be a blessing to all indeed.

You came that we might have life,
Help us Jesus to come against all strife.

Yes, there is still room at the cross,
We trust in God to help us win the loss.

"Can These Bones Live?"

"Can these bones live?" is what I ask,
Yes, if we prophesy and complete the task.
These are my sheep who have gone astray,
Preach the Word to them today.

Tell those bones that God sent His Son,
Let them know Jesus is the only One.
God's Word is powerful and true,
Speak to the valley of bones as God speaks to you.

Just as God breathed into man in the beginning,
He can do it again in the lives of many.
Prophesy to these bones and command them to rise,
Let flesh come on their bones and open their eyes.

Just as the potter kneaded the clay,
Prophesy and let God have His Way.
Can these bones live? I say, "YES",
As the winds blows from the north, east, south and west,
Prophesy and watch God do the rest.

Flying Above the Clouds

As we ascended above the clouds, I thought of how
God lifts us up above our issues in life.
As we ascended the clouds that were once above
us, they are now under us revealing a beautiful blue sky.
This is the power of God that allows us to put the
enemy's tactics under our feet and reveal the beauty of God.

As we reached a certain altitude we
leveled off and moved forward.
Like the stages in our lives.
Through God's Spirit we proceed ahead to the
next level He has for us.

The clouds have shapes like hills and valleys,
reminding us of the times we were in the
valley and God delivered us.
Some clouds look like monuments
reminding us of those things only
God saw us through.

Even as we look down through the clouds, there
are openings giving us a glimpse of where
we were so we don't get big headed
and think we do not need God.

At this height, the things we see look very small
Just like the tests we have gone through victoriously.
Only God can reveal such wonders through
nature and show us our need to remain close to Him.

The sky remains consistently blue,
letting us know that the higher we climb in God
We become stable and unmovable abiding in His Love.

As we continued, the clouds became smooth showing
us what once seemed impossible
has become our floor as we move toward
the next ceiling in our lives.

So, the next time you fly look for these
amazing sights and remember that
God speaks to us in all He has created.

"Living a Kingdom Life"

"But seek ye first the kingdom of God, and his righteousness; and all these things shall be added unto you".
Matthew 6:33 (TLB) KJV

Living a Kingdom life,
Is a life without worry and strife?
Jesus tells us in the Word,
To trust His Father who reigns above.

Acknowledge the Lord in all our ways,
He has promised to bless us all our days.
When we get, weary and don't know the way out,
Trust and believe God's Word and never doubt.

God cares for the fowls of the air that neither sows nor reaps,
How much more does He care for us He promised to keep.
Why do we worry about tomorrow that's not promised to man?
Why not believe God's Word and obey His commands?

When we look at the beauty of the lilies of the field,
How can we not trust God and know that He is real?
The lilies are greater than Solomon and all his glory,
Believe God's Word and the gospel story.

Remove Your Mask

I John 1:5-10 NIV

In Jesus, there is light and not darkness.
Jesus is the light of the world,
When we have Him we have a great pearl.
Serving God is not a great task,
Especially, when we let Him remove our mask;

God is looking for children, who are real,
Trust in God and don't rely on your own zeal.
When we read in the Word of how Jesus died,
What makes us want to deceive and lie?

When we say God so loved the world that He gave,
This should make us want to obey God's Word and behave.
When we live in a world of sin and pain,
All we should do is trust in God and we will gain.

How long will we wear our mask?
It's only what we do honestly for Christ that will last.
Stop! Take inventory from within,
We really can't prosper in sin.

The Bible tells us to examine ourselves in and out,
Don't be in such a hurry to shout.
During this time of revival and renewing our vows,
Let's free ourselves from hypocrisy and be all God has allowed.

Now is the time to "Remove Your Mask"
Because only what we do for Christ will truly last.

"The Kingdom of God is Within Us"

"The Kingdom of God is within you" Luke 17:21b KJV

The kingdom of God must be within every man,
The kingdom is our strength and helps us to obey God's commands.
How can we abide and do God's will?
If we don't let God's kingdom reign in our lives as we remain still.

The gates of hell cannot prevail against the kingdom of God,
We must obey God's and pick up the rod.
When we say, God abides in us,
Obedience to God's word is a must.

God has given us the "power" to tread upon Satan's head.
We don't have to live a life that's useless and dead.
If God's kingdom truly lies within,
Stop allowing the enemy to cause you to sin.

Every excuse was nailed to the cross,
Jesus died that none would be loss.
So, the next time you say God's kingdom is within,
Remember that God has given us the weapons to win.

When we take heed to God's word and take a stand,
We will show God's kingdom to every man.

"You Have Not Seen Anything Yet"

But as it is written: "Eye has not seen, nor ear heard. Nor have entered into the heart of man the things which God has prepared for those who love Him." (I Cor.2:9) NKJV

I will use you in a greater way,
Continue to trust ME and obey.
Your heart is pure concerning souls,
I know that heaven is truly your goal.

You say play me like an instrument almost every day,
I believe that you are being truthful in what you say.
Yield to ME and never stop,
Watch me use you at every bout.

I see your heart and I know it's true,
This is why I have chosen you.
Your heart tells ME to take you back to the way it use to be.
But I have a greater work for thee.

Keep focus stay on track,
Never say how it was and look back.
I will open doors for you,
Stand on MY WORD and preach the truth.

Don't worry about man and their thoughts,
It's you I will use and you I have brought.
Continue to hold on to MY hand,
And I will be with you every time you stand.

I see your heart for the souls of man,
Continue to trust ME and heed my commands.
It's not always what man thinks he permits or lets,
You have not seen anything yet.

"Dwelling in the Secret Place"

Psalm 91:1 NKJV

Lord help me to dwell in the secret place,
Where you become, all I need in this space.
When I sway from where you desire me to be,
Speak to me Lord so I can hear and obey thee.

Help me to trust in you always,
And depend on your guidance all my days.
When the enemy comes in to hinder and try to destroy,
Hide me in the secret place where I trust you and adore.

Help me not to forget who you are and what you spoke,
And not let the enemy make me doubt you and choke.
It is you who speaks truth to my heart,
And it is you who will never depart.

Keep me in the secret place,
And help me to remember this is your race.
Man, has no way to stop what your will is for me,
Help me to stay humble and trust always in thee.

Keep me in the secret place of God,
And help me not to ever depart.
Dwelling in this secret place,
Will keep me focused so that I will finish this race.

Pride

Don't let pride destroy you,
Trust God and He will see you through.
Pride will take you down,
And show you up all over town.

Be who God called you to be,
Pray and allow God to deliver thee.
Don't let the enemy destroy you from within,
Trust in God and you will always win.

Pride is a dangerous weapon that makes you feel like you should fight,
But God, will take you through and give you His sight.
Surrender to God's will for your life,
Because it's without pain or strife.

Pride, put it under your feet,
Allow God to bless you as you become meek.
Your winning is in letting go,
Keeping your victory as you close the door.

Acronyms

Access

Accepting God's will for thee

Christ gave his life at Calvary

Christ is the only way

Everlasting peace He gives today

Sin no longer has dominion over me

Salvation through Jesus who died that I might be free

Challenge

Challenges in life we will have, that's a fact

Hope in God; don't let it be an act

Always know God's voice

Leaning on Him for every choice

Love is His name

Everlasting to everlasting He remains the same

New beginnings He gives each day

Guiding us every step of the way

Eternal life is ours today

Jesus

Jesus is the only way
Ever interceding for us each day
Saved us from a world of sin
Unity in Him is the only way to win
Salvation He gave accept it now

May God's blessings ever be yours.

(

Printed in the United States
by Baker & Taylor Publisher Services